HAZARDS OF A
HANDYMAN

C. W. REES

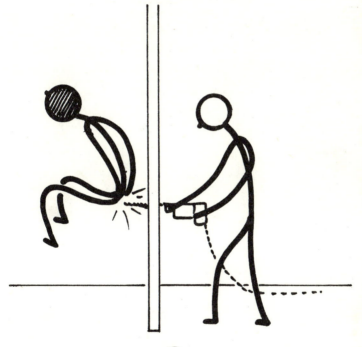

Paul Elek London

© C. W. Rees, 1973

First published in 1973 in Great Britain by
ELEK BOOKS LIMITED
54-58 Caledonian Road
London N1 9RN

ISBN 0 236 15484 2

Printed in England by
Weatherby Woolnough Limited
Sanders Road, Wellingborough, Northants. NN8 4BX

CONTENTS

To those who would, but dare not.
To those who dare, but should not.

Introduction

The *true* Handyman is a rare fish indeed, and let no one imagine otherwise.

The fact that you have this book in your hands indicates either that you are unlikely to be one yourself, or that you have a morbid curiosity and should do something about it. On the other hand, of course, you could have picked up the book because it was the only one available, or you might be buying it for someone else, or someone might have left a lurid book-jacket on it by mistake.

Certainly, men do exist who are dexterous with tools and brimming with ideas who can transform tea-chests into radiograms and radiograms into bathroom cabinets without bringing down the ceiling or losing a finger. But they are the extremely rare fish I referred to, and have nothing to do with us.

These men apart, the *handyman* is the greatest confidence trick since 'the apple'. A trick which has been perpetrated by housewives down through the ages from Eve to Elizabeth, or whatever your wife's name may be. And with such cunning and calculation have they schemed that we men, even the more shrewd ones, have never had a clue.

Even those astute members of our sex (and by now you will have guessed to which sex we belong) who are capable of manipulating vast armies on the battlefield, or assembling, single-handed, the most complicated computer, or standing up in court and arguing the intricacies of a libel action, or with deft fingers removing a ducal gallstone – are as children in the hands of the Pied Piper when their wives start plotting their downfall.

Their schemes are conceived (and the fertility rate is high) over the bone-china coffee cups in a Mayfair flat, or around the Sub-Committee's table at the Women's Institute, or panting up the concrete steps in The Flats when the lift has packed in.

Someone has only to boast about the simply marvellous cocktail cabinet that Geoffrey made out of the grand piano that no one played any more; or how Arthur converted the outside toilet into an aviary; or about the smashing cupboard Fred put under the sink to store the empties in – and the seed is sown. Nature, as human as ever was, can safely be relied upon to do the rest.

Whether Geoffrey, Arthur or Fred were the true stars of these domestic extravaganzas, or whether they had the assistance of suitable craftsmen, or merely supervised the activities of those craftsmen, or, indeed, were only contemplating the possibility of one of these ventures – the damage is done. The picture has been formed in the mind of the listener who hurries home determined never again to be unable to compete in such a conversation – if, indeed, she can wait until such a conversation arises.

Choosing her moment with a skill which only dedication and experience could beget, she regales her husband with a detailed and possibly exaggerated account of these hearsay achievements. This is followed (again prompted by past experience) by flattering him into the conviction that he is capable of even greater things, or shaming him into wishing he was, and sparking off a determination to find out.

It never fails. We men are gullible creatures – vain, too. And how quickly the members of the opposite sex learn how to exploit our weaknesses. This is one of the first lessons they learn at their mother's knees – how to bring us to ours.

It's not long after the opening gambit that she decides what miracle she wants wrought in the home, and, in next to no time, she is boasting to her associates of its progress, and with as much enthusiasm and as little regard for the truth as the friends who inspired her.

For *they* did not allow the true facts to dim the brightness of their sagas. Geoffrey's wife, for instance, omitted to mention that when they have guests they leave the bottles casually on top of the cocktail cabinet because they never have been able to open its doors. Arthur's wife remained silent about the birds who were drowned because somehow or other the overflow, which had been made redundant, overflowed. And Fred's missus forgot about the door which is superfluous because the side of the cupboard never would stay on.

But our victim is hooked. Having either succumbed to flattery as he has done before, or surrendered to a direct onslaught which past experience ensured he would, he sets about propping up his wife's honour with whatever tools time and necessity have so far provided.

And so another 'handyman' is launched upon an un-suspecting world. Had there existed even the slightest aptitude for the rough and tumble of *make and mend,* he would already have been in at the deep end, keen and

11

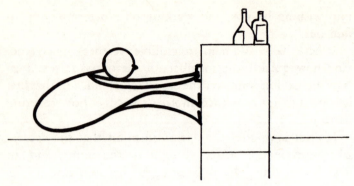

'Never been able to open the doors'

enthusiastic, not shivering on the bank waiting for the shove that's as inevitable as the splash heralding his undignified beginnings.

His heart isn't in it from the start, and only his wife's relentless drive will divorce him from his television chair or deprive him of his evening trip to the 'local', goading him on to risk body, limb and sanity in an unequal conflict with what was all right to start with, anyway.

There are many such unfortunates in the world, and many more in the making; innocent and unaware of the ensnaring mesh surrounding them. It is for them that this book has been written in the pious hope that it may be instrumental in sparing them some of the suffering and anguish of those who have trod the thorny path before.

In the past, husbands not wishing to become involved in household repairs and transformations, have offered the excuses of lack of tools, materials and know-how. But the tools and materials have always appeared with predictable certainty, and the husbands have been obliged to face their problems with a complete ignorance of how to use the tools (even if the materials aroused no terror) and an embarrassing lack of know-how.

That is the gap this book is designed to fill – the use of the tools and the know-how. For lack of familiarity with either creates the hazards referred to. And while these hazards do not, in themselves, threaten civilisation as we know it, they can be painful, expensive and regrettable.

But I must make it quite clear from the outset that in no circumstances can I, or my heirs or assigns, accept any responsibility whatsoever, arising from any advice given or believed to have been given, which may result, directly or indirectly, in the estrangement of husband and wife or the destruction, in part or whole, of any messuage or dwelling in which the said husband and wife resided when the accident occurred.

It is just as well to get this clear before proceeding, since a neighbour who enquired about converting his electric wiring to ring-circuit – but that is another story. And in any case, his widow has now settled out of court.

Perhaps this is the point at which one piece of sound, irrefutable advice should be offered to the man faced with his first domestic challenge. It is offered, not with any hope that it will be accepted, but with the firm conviction that it should be.

It is this. *Botch it!*

Make a complete and utter mess of the job so that your wife will be convinced, once and for all, that your talents must lie in other directions, and that renovations and

'destruction . . . of any . . . dwelling'

innovations in the future should be left to the little man down the road with the notice over his door claiming to be capable of all the things she had in mind for you – well, *almost* all.

The person with the courage to take this advice is not only brave but wise, and is set fair to enjoy a longer life, an unmutilated body, an absence of grey hair, and the joy of not being haunted by the spectre of uncompleted tasks, so mercilessly resurrected during domestic disputes.

But few, if any, will heed.

So, with colours and tails well down, they will *try* to be handymen. They will give up their Saturday afternoon football and Sunday morning naps, and the television will see them no more. They will wear their oldest suits interminably and a smile hardly ever. Their turn-ups will be filled with sawdust instead of fluff, their cigarette bill will double and their fingers will take turns to be bandaged.

And they will *still* botch the jobs – but unintentionally.

Fortunately, you don't need to be one of them – not entirely. That is why this book has been written. To place in your hands a fund of knowledge they do not enjoy. To afford you timely warning of the hazards that line the handyman's path, and so enable you to pick your steps a little more discerningly.

You may still have to make the sacrifices they make, and suffer as they suffer – that is the inseparable lot of the handyman. But the odds against the task you undertake becoming an expensive calamity will be a little shorter – a little!

Any newcomer to an art or craft is bound to make mistakes. The prime object of this book is to enable you to make your first errors between its covers, and not all over the house. So that, in effect, you pass from the apprentice to the improver stage with the minimum loss of time, temper, blood and dignity.

Read on, then, and good luck to you.

One

The Tools

The majority of jobs about the house are executed (and the word is more often justified than not) with a saw, a hammer, a bag of assorted nails, and little else.

While it is quite true that much can be accomplished with such simple equipment, and far be it from me to decry their undoubted versatility, life can be made easier and grief shorter by a few supplementary aids. These need not be numerous if well chosen, and a little space devoted to them and their uses will enable you to know what to try to borrow from your neighbours when the need arises.

Of course, you may be unfortunate in your neighbours, in which case you are faced with two choices – either to *buy* the tools you need or to move to another neighbourhood where your luck may change.

As this chapter is about *tools,* even the two already mentioned, although they are common to most households, are referred to again since some uncommon households still exist.

The Hammer

The hammer and its uses are so well known that to make specific mention of it may seem superfluous; but, as already suggested, it is unwise to take anything for granted, even a hammer.

The main purpose of a hammer is to concentrate force on a pre-selected spot, and the fact that the hammer and its user select different spots disproves nothing.

By this means the domestic hammer usually knocks nails into things or, sometimes, out of things. But the hammer is a versatile instrument and during its lifetime is called upon to play many parts, all of them noisy. It is used to loosen things which are tight and to tighten things which are loose – like a water-tap, a door-bolt, a beer-barrel bung or the handle of another hammer.

It can be used to open swollen windows or doors, stubborn tin-lids, brazil nuts and piggy-banks. It can be used to create or destroy, to straighten or to bend, to flatten or to dent, to attract attention or express displeasure, and is, perhaps, the most individually successful tool of all.

There are various kinds of hammers, all of them unkind. Their very nature is violent and they never fail to bring out the worst in their users – particularly bad blood. They hurt most the ones who use them, except when employed as blunt instruments.

Hammers are rarely ever the right size. They are usually too small to hit the nail but too big to miss the finger. As a rough guide (and only experience will prove how rough) for large nails you need a big hammer and for small nails a small hammer. The reason for this is fairly obvious, but for any who have not yet caught up, it should be explained that because a panel pin is very small and difficult to hold you use a smaller hammer so that it doesn't hurt as much.

Considering the infinite variety of nails which exist you might think this would entail having an infinite variety of hammers, but it doesn't. You make do with what you have – and an infinite variety of contusions.

One very useful type of hammer – or would be useful if it worked – has a head with a striking surface on one side and a claw formation on the other for removing unwanted nails, they say. But when the salesman is demonstrating the use of this particular model you will notice that the nail is always sticking well out of the wood so that he can easily slide the claw under its head, while the nail *you* need to remove will always be firmly buried right up to its scalp.

They* tell you to hold the hammer at the end of its handle. If you do you will find that you are too far from the nail especially if your eyesight is bad. They say that such a grip gives more power to your blow, but who wants to be on the receiving end of a more powerful blow?

You must please yourself, of course, but the short grip is much more intimate and gentle, and less damage is likely to be done when the head flies off the handle.

When hammering a nail, the line of force should always be identical with the line of the nail itself. Any deviation to right or left will result in one of two things. Either the hammer will slide off the head of the nail causing severe bruising to the work or worker, or the nail will bend into a shape varying from a gentle curve to an inverted letter 'U'.

In the first case deal with the bruise as best you can and

* 'They' refers to most other text books already written on the subject.

try again. In the second case you have two choices.

You can either extract the nail and begin again or, by carefully aimed blows, continue to drive the nail on its new parabolic course.

The latter is an adventure that most people embark upon at some time or other, as thousands of scars from nails which have collapsed at the waist will testify to. So be warned and plump for removing the nail and starting again.

During recent years the familiar wooden handle has gradually been replaced by a rubber one which provides a better grip, is warmer to hold in the winter and is useful for making corrections to wörking-drawings. But there will be many occasions when you will wish the change had taken place in the head rather than the handle.

As with most tools, the hammer should be kept safely away from the inquisitive hands of small children. But, unlike other tools, this is not because the children are liable to injure themselves with it – this they never seem to do – but because they have an instinct for selecting your most treasured possession on which to prove that the use of the hammer comes as naturally to a five-year-old as the use of a corkscrew to his father.

The Pincers

It is only right that the pincers should come immediately after the hammer because in practice that is exactly what occurs. Even so, they are mentioned almost apologetically, because although they are always included in every craftsman's tool kit, they are not a tool of which anyone is inordinately proud. Like the typist's eraser, the pincers are for correcting mistakes, so their use is nothing to boast about.

Their purpose is to remove the nail that shouldn't have been there in the first place.

In theory, the jaws of the pincers should close on the offending nail just beneath its head, gripping the neck firmly. Then, with a steady, upward pull (but more frequently an impatient rocking movement which doubles the mouth of the hole the nail created) the nail is removed.

That's the theory. But in practice the task is complicated by the fact that the person responsible for the nail's predicament (no names) excelled in his indiscretion and buried the nail deep in its hiding-place, making it improbable that the pincers can ever come to grips with it.

Even when they can manage to grip the nail they have a tendency to bite off the head. And if you've ever had your head bitten off you can imagine how co-operative the nail is likely to be after that.

One word of warning. Always keep both hands as far from the jaws as the length of the pincers will allow. Any temptation, however worthy, to assist the jaws to locate their target can be fatal. Well, perhaps 'fatal' is an exaggeration, but, be assured, when you have been nipped by a pair of pincers you will be in no mood to split hairs over exaggerations.

The Screwdriver

The screwdriver is closely allied to the hammer since its

main purpose is to assist in the union of two pieces of wood (or other material, or one of each, or any combination of them) and sometimes to assist in their divorce. Its use is, in fact, mainly restricted to driving screws *in* or coaxing screws *out*. Into or out of *what* matters little since the drill is the same.

There are various sizes of screwdrivers, large ones for use against large screws and small ones for small screws. Although most people manage with only one, which accounts for its peculiar shape and the number of screws left jutting above the surface. But these can always be trimmed off with a hacksaw or camouflaged with ragged material or torn flesh.

They say you should use the longest screwdriver which the space you are working in will permit. In theory this is supposed to increase power and keep the blade in the screw-slot. But in practice you are too far away from the screw to know whether the other end is in the slot or not, so that you are liable to go on turning for a long time without effect, and fritter away all the increased power you could well have done without.

The screwdriver is used by placing the blade end into the screw-slot and turning in a clockwise direction to drive the screw home, and anti-clockwise to remove it. That is, providing the screw will stand up long enough for you to insert the screwdriver if you are screwing it in, and providing the screw has any intention of budging if you are trying to remove it.

Sometimes a screw will be so stubborn that no matter how hard you try, the screwdriver will be unable to turn it. Indications that you have met one of these will arrive in the shape of a large blister in the palm of your hand. Occasionally such a screw will react to violence. Place the blade of the screwdriver in the slot of the screw and hit the handle smartly with a hammer. Even if it doesn't work it will relieve your feelings.

But whatever happens don't blame the screwdriver – unless it was the one that put the screw there in the first place.

There are various types of screwdrivers and perhaps one of the most useful is the 'ratchet' screwdriver, which enables you to continue turning for long periods without removing your hand from the handle, if you have a taste for that sort of thing.

The ratchet can be set in forward, reverse or neutral gear, according to whether you are inserting the screw, withdrawing it, or merely ruminating. But make sure *how* it is set before you begin, or the article you are working on may fall apart as the screwdriver whips out all the screws you intended to drive home.

Apart from its normal uses, a screwdriver is handy for levering lids off paint-tins, testing sparking plugs, changing tyres, stirring tea and paint (but not together), opening oysters, and holding down the tongue to examine tonsils.

The Saw

This is a tool without which any job is better not started, unless you are accomplished at karate.

A saw is a cutting tool with teeth, and a partiality for blood rather than sawdust. This should be borne in mind

Jig-saw

at all times, thus making it unnecessary for the saw to remind you.

Saws are made in an endless variety and their sizes and patterns are as varied as their uses are confusing. A craftsman would not dream of making a particular kind of cut except with a particular saw, even though half a dozen others would do as well, and it is by your ability to guess which that your stature will be measured.

The sizes of saw vary from the most delicate ones for extremely fine work to the most savage ones for devouring whole trees. And in between stretches a cavalcade of alternatives which do not take into account circular saws, jig-saws, bandsaws and fretsaws.

The larger the saw the more terrifying the teeth, so that it would come as no suprise should the bigger ones eventually be sold complete with first-aid kits and artificial fingers.

Some saws are used for sawing wood and nothing else – unless the wood happens to contain a hidden nail. On contact with the nail it will cry out in anguish, but ignore it. The saw should not be encouraged to make a fuss about the presence of a foreign body. Racial prejudice has no place in the home workshop.

If you do not happen to have a workshop be warned that saws are not very intelligent and are totally incapable of differentiating between the wood you are sawing and the dining-table on which the wood is resting. So keep a wary eye on the sawdust. When it changes colour you have gone too far, but if it turns red, you've gone *much* too far.

When making the first incision you should rest the saw against the first finger of the left hand (provided the saw is held in your right hand) so that should the saw jump it will catch your finger and not mutilate the wood you are cutting.

If, while sawing, the stroke becomes gradually stiffer, it may be that the saw needs greasing, or that you have changed direction slightly and the saw is unwilling to bend to it, or the wood itself is not properly seasoned, or, and it is more than likely, you are sawing through the table again.

One drawback with a saw is the noise it makes – but only when in use. It is loud and monotonous and makes sawing in secret impossible. But unless your window has bars there is probably no reason why you should want to.

Nevertheless, it is a sound which is rarely enjoyed by family or neighbours, so get that part of the work over as quickly as possible or drown it with loud music.

When sawing along a pencilled line, and this is a good habit to form, you will find that the sawdust will persist in obliterating the line. The way to prevent this is to saw in the opposite direction. If for any reason, this is not practicable, you can do what the less particular craftsmen do and blow it away. But should you still be working on the table the sawdust is liable to get into the food.

Accuracy requires that the piece of wood you are sawing should be held perfectly still. This is best achieved by placing your free hand firmly on one end and your knee on the other. This may present problems if the piece of wood is very small or you are still working on that table – unless of course you happen to be a different shape from other people.

It should always be remembered that the blade of a saw has a thickness, and allowance should be made for this when working to exact dimensions. Failure to do so has produced more bad joints than arthritis has.

The Plane

The purpose of a plane is to reduce the size of a piece of wood. A saw, of course, does much the same thing in a different way and more quickly.

But whereas the saw reduces the length or width of the wood, the plane reduces its thickness. Naturally, if you buy the wood the right size in the first place you won't need either.

But supposing you have bought the wood, taken it home, discovered it is too thick and don't like to take it back to the shop – then you will definitely need a plane. Should you discover the wood is too thin – bad luck!

The theory of planing is that a thin slice (called a 'shaving') is removed from the wood at each excursion of the plane over its surface, the plane being pushed by the right hand and guided by the left. But it's what happens between the two hands that really matters, and there seems no way of controlling that, or very little. And even controlling it in theory, which, after all, is what we are discussing.

The blade of the plane can be adjusted, with a turn of the screwdriver, a few taps of the hammer, and the usual misgivings, so that it either slides over the wood leaving no sign of its passing other than an increased shine, or digs its cutting edge into the grain and refuses to budge. Somewhere between these two positions lies a happy medium which some have sought all their lives without discovering.

But supposing you are lucky – or clever if you like – and produce the desired thickness of shaving, from there on it doesn't matter how careful you are, one part of the surface will always end up lower than the rest. In trying to rectify this the wood will gradually become too thin, and back to the shop you go for more wood. So you needn't have bought the plane after all.

Nor need this result be achieved only through *bad* planing. The very act of planing with its smooth, rhythmic movement has a hypnotic effect which can easily

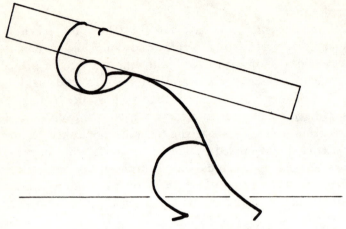

'don't like to take it back to the shop'

produce a transcendental stupor from which only the complete disappearance of the wood, or the telephone bell, or opening time, can arouse you.

If you are one of the fortunates able to use the plane successfully you will find that the pocket which houses the blade eventually becomes filled with shavings which should be removed frequently to make room for more. Failure to do this will result in a congestion that is resented by the plane which packs up until the proper treatment has been administered. In serious cases this entails delicate probing with the point of a pencil (which always breaks), a nail file (which is never available), or a bradawl (which does more harm than good).

'Opening time'

One thing to be said in favour of the plane is that it is a fairly safe tool. You really have to fool around to cut yourself with it because the cutting edge is so well hidden, in fact no one should cut himself with a plane – a saw is much easier.

Like all other tools, planes come in a variety of sizes, and whatever size you buy, the one you need is always the one you almost bought.

The Chisel

A rough description of a chisel (very rough) would be

that it is like a miniature plane with a long wooden handle. And while it can be pushed like a plane for delicate work, it is more usually knocked with a hammer or preferably a mallet, which is a wooden hammer with a big head and little justification.

Owing to this latter method of use a chisel is a double source of danger to its user – the cutting edge at one end and the mallet at the other makes it extremely difficult to know which to watch.

It is used for making square holes, oblong holes, slots, cavities and generally removing unwanted wood from wanted wood in small chunks, and would be invaluable if only it knew when to stop. It is also beloved of wives for sharpening pencils, replacing lost sardine-tin keys, removing tacks from linoleum and drawing pins from anywhere.

Although intended for work on wood the chisel cares little what it digs into – so look out!

Owing to its capacity for going wrong it has lent its name to certain types of fraud, as in 'chiselling'.

Chisels vary in size from small ones which can be pressed into service as emergency screwdrivers but are never the same again, to large ones which can also remove wallpaper, not to mention divots of plaster.

There is one type called a 'cold' chisel which is not used on wood but is employed to make holes in brickwork, concrete or petty cash boxes. It is so called because it doesn't have a wooden handle and is unpleasant to hold during the winter months. This chisel is never used with a mallet since the mallet would make no impression on it, but this is not true vice versa. It is always used with

'removing unwanted wood'

a hammer which not only makes more noise but slips easily off the head of the chisel and adds colour to the atmosphere.

In use, the head of the hammer bounces on the head of the chisel and the blade of the chisel bounces on the brickwork or concrete making it almost impossible to keep to the dimensions of the hole you originally had in mind. Consequently, always start with a smaller hole than you require and hope to stop in time.

There are also chisels with rounded blades called gouges. Despite their name they are not used for removing eyeballs unless the user is particularly careless. Their purpose is to produce a fluted effect. They require much skill and are best left to addicts.

The Bradawl

One tool always to be found in a craftsman's kit – well, always included but not always to be found – is a bradawl. In shape it is very similar to a screwdriver, and very often used as one. But this is not its purpose.

Its blade is not as tough as that of the screwdriver and it quickly loses heart in conflct with a screw which shows the slightest resistance.

It is intended for making small holes in wood and this it does without creating shavings or sawdust which, when you think of it, is really quite clever.

But the resulting hole is rarely an end in itself. Rather is it the beginning of a bigger hole. It is an 'encourager', like the carrot held before the donkey, making life easier for a nail, a screw, a drill or a cuphook.

The hole it makes is rarely deep enough. But if you make it deep enough you cannot remove the bradawl, so it's best to compromise.

Sometimes it is used for marking a line in the absence of a pencil, but in this it must be used with discretion as the resulting mark cannot be rubbed out.

It is also good for making holes in paper, but be careful what is underneath as the bradawl is, by nature, insensitive.

You will find it useful, too, for removing shavings from a plane or planting seeds, and in emergency it will serve as a hat-and-coat hook, doorstop or pipe-cleaner.

The Brace-and-Bit

In any conversation on making holes the name 'brace-and-bit' is sure to crop up sooner or later. So why not now!

A brace-and-bit is a most useful tool for making round holes in almost anything. (Notice 'brace-and-bit', contrary to expectations, is treated as singular. This is because they've been together now for well, a pretty long time and as either without the other would be useless they are treated as 'one'.)

A brace can be used with an assortment of bits for making holes of different sizes. But try and decide upon the right one as soon as possible as too many holes may weaken the material you are working on.

There are many different kinds of bits, a description of which would only prove confusing – to both of us. In the end, the purpose of each is the same – to make a hole –

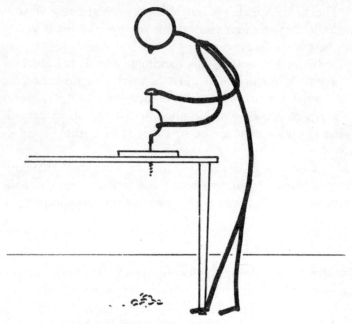

'working on the dining-table'

and the difference mainly one of size and finesse.

The brace-and-bit is a reasonably safe tool to use under normal circumstances, unless you still happen to be working on the dining-table. But even then the holes are useful for brushing crumbs through.

The secret of successful boring is to keep the bit at right angles to the work. When drilling horizontally this can best be achieved by resting the handle end against the chest or stomach, depending upon the position of the hole or the condition of the driller. But in any case, be sure it *is* the handle end. An error can prove both painful and draughty.

When drilling vertically the drill can be steadied by resting the forehead on the hand on top of the brace. But this attitude together with the rhythmic turning of the brace is conducive to slumber and some caution should be observed.

Should there be a reluctance on the part of the bit to penetrate the wood, this can be due to one of three things. The wood may be very hard, the bit may be very blunt, or you have forgotten to fit a bit into the brace.

In the first case change the wood or press on; in the second case borrow a sharper one; in the third case – wake up!

When boring you will find that as the bit penetrates the timber a spiral of wood emerges from the hole. This has no commercial value and can safely be thrown away.

The Electric Drill

The whole role of the handyman has been revolutionised by the introduction of the electric drill. The tool, as its name implies, is designed to drill holes, but it does this with such terrifying speed that any job can be ruined by just one moment of indecision. The whole secret of success is knowing not only when to stop but how to transfer the thought from your brain to your finger on the trigger in time.

The electric drill is nothing if not wilful. You may mark the desired position of the hole as clearly as you like, with pencil, biro, or anything you choose, but the hole itself will

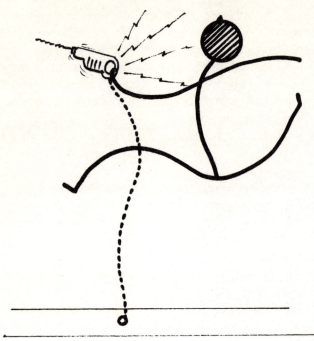

'not properly earthed'

still materialise to the left or right, or above or below, leaving your mark completely unsullied. This demands adaptability on the part of the handyman who should be able to modify his plans accordingly.

One side-effect of the electric drill has been a boom in the art world occasioned by a growing demand for pictures to cover unwanted holes in walls.

When drilling a wall the deposits on the bit (plaster,

breeze, brick, concrete) will frequently indicate how far you have penetrated. If the bit, when withdrawn, bears traces of marmalade – you have penetrated your neighbour's larder.

Before drilling wood vertically (especially on a table) read the paragraph under the heading 'The Brace-and-Bit' which commences 'The brace-and-bit is a reasonably safe tool. . . '. The effect is the same only much quicker.

It is of the utmost importance (and this applies equally to the brace-and-bit) to select with care the size of bit you require for the particular job you have in hand. It is almost impossible to reduce the size of a hole once made, and it isn't always convenient to start all over again. If you have the time you may not have the wood if you have the alternative bit.

Many accessories are available to convert the drill to any number of other uses. It can be adapted to saw, grind, polish and give electric shocks if not properly earthed.

It can also wake babies, scare cats, annoy neighbours, and ruin television programmes if not adequately suppressed.

Always switch off the drill before laying it down, unless you like your furniture different or you have little regard for your landlord. This applies particularly when the drill is adapted for sawing or sanding.

The Square
This is a most depressing instrument as its only purpose is to confirm how untrue your work is. It is used chiefly by masochistic carpenters.

It can be made of all wood, or metal, or part wood and

part metal, but its message is just as uncharitable.

Apart from testing work already done it can be applied to work to *be* done. It will enable a line to be drawn at right angles to the edge of any piece of wood which will successfully defy any saw to follow it.

It is equally willing to indicate how far out of true your joints are – long before they fall apart.

The Spirit Level

This has nothing to do with the breathaliser test. In fact, it should be more truthfully named a *Dis*pirit Level, as it is rarely the bearer of any news but bad.

Like the square it is another gadget to fill the handy-man with negative thoughts and should be abandoned before being purchased.

Its sole purpose is to tell you that the left-hand side should be higher or the right-hand side lower, and if you are happier without that knowledge – why bother?

They come in all sizes – if you let them.

They rely on the theory that a bubble of air imprisoned in a tube of liquid will always rise to the highest point. But anything incarcerated for any length of time is capable of the most unpredictable excursions, so the theory seems to be based on an extremely flimsy premise.

The spirit level's only justifiable use is for testing other people's work.

Nails

Without doubt nails are the handyman's best friend.

NAILS . . .

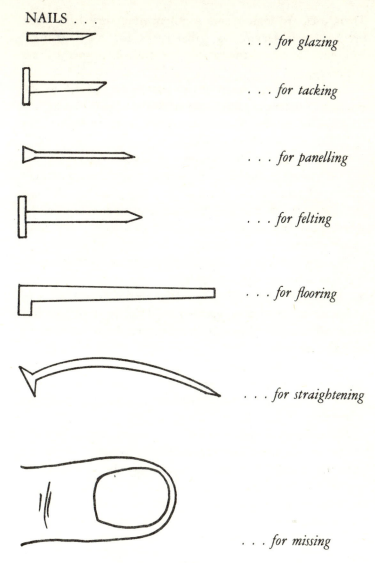

. . . *for glazing*

. . . *for tacking*

. . . *for panelling*

. . . *for felting*

. . . *for flooring*

. . . *for straightening*

. . . *for missing*

Their uses are legion and in their time they have been pressed into service as substitutes for most things, including some of the skills that craftsmen spend years acquiring.

They have been used instead of glue, halved joints, mortise and tenon joints, dovetail joints, dowels, screws, coat-hooks, bradawls, cribbage pegs, cup-hooks and, in extremity, even trouser-buttons.

Sometimes nails are used not as a substitute for joints but to reinforce them. This is only when the craftsman lacks confidence in his work. On these occasions the nails are driven below the surface with a 'nail punch' and the recess filled in with plastic wood to conceal the poor man's shame.

Do not feel discouraged if you experience difficulty in hitting a nail straight – or, for that matter, hitting it at all. Over the years nails have developed a perverseness of character which makes 'going straight' a dirty phrase, but the angle and direction of their waywardness varies from nail to nail.

After all, if hammering a nail was a simple procedure there would be little point in saying 'you've hit the nail on the head' when someone makes an unusually profound statement.

Some nails are more exasperating than others. They will allow you to drive them home perfectly, right up to the last quarter-inch, then they suddenly lay their heads along the wood as though it were the executioner's block, and the next blow of your hammer leaves an ugly scar on the wood where head and neck have sunk horizontally into it. This inevitably happens on the most prominent part of whatever you are making.

Screws

It is but a very short step from nails to screws since, like nails, they are used for joining things together but in cases where it may be necessary at some future date to take them apart – if they haven't come apart of their own accord in the meantime.

Like nails they vary in size and length, from the very little ones which are easy to lose to the very large ones which are almost impossible to turn.

In use, they start off willingly enough and then seem to regret their co-operation, resisting every further effort to turn them. They have probably been responsible for more tender hands and tough language than anything else in the carpenter's tool-box.

Screws are chiefly made of either iron or brass but can be made of almost any metal and usually are.

There are three main types – countersunk, raised-heads and round-heads. They each have their particular uses but it is customary to use whatever you've got.

Having selected your screw you will probably find that it is just that little bit longer than the thickness of the wood you are working on so that it sticks out the other side about a quarter of an inch. You must then decide whether to waste time hunting for another screw or just hope that no one will tear their trousers/tights/jeans/dress/skirt on it.

If you experience difficulty in driving home a screw, wait until you try to *un*screw one, an old one which has

41

been painted – many times.

You will probably be too far advanced with the job to abandon it so you will need to press on. When you have tried using a mallet on the screwdriver in vain, and scarred all the surrounding paintwork with the darting blade, and bandaged the blister on your hand, you have one last resort, a red-hot iron.

You place it on the head of the reluctant screw and hold it there until the smoke dies down. This will either loosen the screw through the heat, or raise a blister on the surrounding paintwork to match the one on your hand. Either way, you've tried.

Before commencing a job where screws are to be used always ensure that you have at least three times as many as you think you will need. Screws have a propensity for falling either out of the hole or from your fingers, and when they fall they roll in the most impossible directions and finally disappear never to be seen again.

Some day someone will make a fortune by discovering their hiding-place.

The Gluepot

Although not so much in evidence these days the gluepot still adds that professional touch to any workshop. It doesn't even have to be used, merely to stand around looking dark and mysterious.

It is not such a great mystery really. It consists of two metal pots, one fitting inside the other. The larger and lower one contains water (if someone has remembered to fill it – and this is only possible if the two can be separated) and into the other, pieces of cake glue are placed. The whole apparatus is placed on the fire or gas-ring, and when the water gets hot it heats and melts the glue and fills the neighbourhood with the foulest smell this side of a tannery.

However, since the introduction of various types of glue in tubes few people now use the gluepot – except to give tone to their workshops and to annoy the neighbours.

The Blowlamp

The blowlamp is a very useful instrument if you succeed in lighting it. If you fail to light it the thing is useless, but you and your loved ones may well start counting your blessings.

While being ignited it always manages to look and sound dangerous – it is.

In use, blowlamps are given to duplicity, since although they burn with a considerable roar, their flame, especially in a strong light, is almost invisible. Once having become accustomed to the noise, discomfort is just around the corner.

When you put a blowlamp down always remember where, and particularly which side the handle is.

In effect it is a miniature flame-thrower intended for burning old paint off wooden surfaces before repainting – unless you happen to be plumbing, when this isn't true at all.

It is capable of cracking windows or setting fire to curtains with equal indifference. When burning off paint

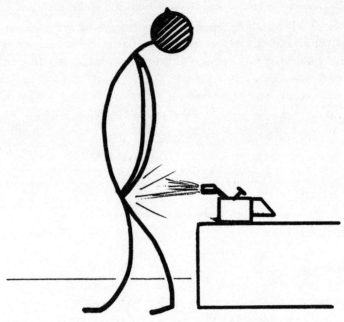

'their flame . . . is almost invisible'

do not concentrate on one spot too long or you may discover that that dark area isn't paint at all, especially when it begins to glow.

A blowlamp should never be pointed at a friend or a close relative from whom there are expectations. Professional painters can sometimes be seen lighting cigarettes in the flame, but this is not to be recommended to the handyman unless he wishes to go through life, like the professional, eyebrowless.

An alternative to the blowlamp is a stripper – but this

may incur domestic displeasure, and, in any case, it will do you more good to get on with the job.

Brushes

The first brush that comes to mind is, of course, the paint-brush. Never economise on paintbrushes. Make it an inflexible rule always to use the best possible brushes you can borrow.

Another excellent rule is always to ensure that brushes are thoroughly cleaned after use so that they are immediately ready for the next job. A discreet hint to your neighbour should be sufficient.

Always have as wide a variety of sizes available as possible. To try to paint a large surface with a one-inch brush is tedious, to say the least; while to paint the narrow glazing bars of a window with a four-inch brush will darken the room appreciably.

When painting, it is more economical to dip only the bristles in the paint. After all, the paint that runs down your arm is travelling in the wrong direction.

Your strokes should be firm and rhythmic, and made in the direction indicated by the bristles left behind in the previous painting. Keeping the paint-tin near the area being painted saves running back and fore, economises on paint, and reduces cleaning bills.

Hold the brush by the wooden handle only. It is much less messy, especially when the paint is low in the tin.

Besides the brushes used for painting there are others with their own specific uses. Like the *whitewash-brush* which is large and heavy enough to slow you down when

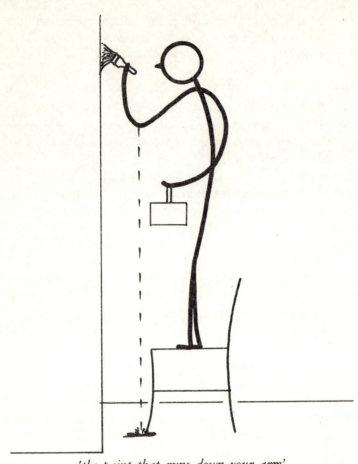

'*the paint that runs down your arm*'

whitening a ceiling and so prevents you from skimping the work.

There is the *paste-brush* used for applying paste to wall-paper (on the unpatterned side). This is large and heavy, too, like the whitewash brush and for the same reason. Usually it's the same brush.

The *glue-brush* is quite small as you would expect of a brush which frequently has to negotiate small apertures. It is usually left in the gluepot as it is a menace anywhere else. But when the glue in the gluepot sets, don't try to remove the brush; only the handle will respond.

Then there is the *dusting-brush* used for removing dust from the surface you are about to paint and depositing it on the surface you will paint next, or, more than likely, on the part you have just painted.

Finally, there is the *sweeping-brush,* left conveniently in the vicinity of your work by your wife. It is left without comment but never fails to convey its message.

The Paint-Strainer

While on the subject of painting, mention should be made of the paint-strainer. You will find, if you have not discovered already, that you have only to take your eyes away from an open tin of paint for a moment for a skin to form over its surface. If this is stirred into the paint it will show up in ugly little scars on your painted surface.

To avoid this the paint is poured through the paint-strainer which completely removes the skin – together with an appreciable quantity of paint. The process of straining becomes slower and slower over the years as the

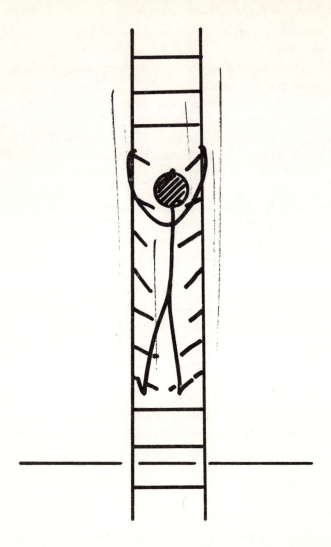

'*the return journey may well be fraught with surprises*'

strainer fills up with skin.

A very good substitute for a strainer can be made with an old silk or nylon stocking. But ensure the leg is removed first or, at least, pushed well to one side.

The Ladder

Unless you are exceptionally tall there will be many occasions when you will find a ladder useful if not indispensable.

Before using it, have the strength of the rungs tested, preferably by someone heavier than yourself. Although this always leaves behind the disquieting thought that his weight may have been the last but one straw – and you still have to use it.

Also check that all the rungs are there. Passing a gap on the way up can usually be accomplished successfully but the return journey may well be fraught with surprises.

If you climb to the top of a tall ladder and find you have no head for heights – well, you've got no one to blame but yourself. It is worse still, of course, if you should lose your nerve and are unable to descend. It can become very lonely up there.

When erecting a ladder do not have the foot too near the base of the wall. It may take up less room but it becomes difficult to climb and even more difficult to stay on.

If halfway up you get the sensation that the ladder is swaying, don't worry – it is.

It is on ladders that bandy-legged people come into their own since it is much easier to climb with one knee

'The sensation that the ladder is swaying'

on either side of the uprights. The extra grip it affords easily outweighs the discomfort of an occasional splinter.

When you have completed the area you are working on and wish to move the ladder to the next, always come down the ladder first. It saves time in the long run.

Before climbing a ladder make sure you know how many rungs there are. It is embarrassing to go too far.

These, then, are some of the tools with which a handyman should be familiar. Perhaps *familiar* is not the ideal word but let's not be pernickety. There are many more tools but these should leave you with sufficient problems for now.

Two

Acquiring the Tools

You are now acquainted with the tools, or some of the tools, without which you have successfully lived your life so far, but which suddenly become as indispensable as that lawnmower you didn't want either.

How you acquire your own set of tools is a matter of personal decision. Your wife's – not yours. Not that you will be aware of this distinction, either at the time or even later. The tools will appear from time to time as the result of subtle suggestions, or in the form of presents, or unmissable bargains, or through coupons cut from papers, or what have you.

But come they will, and ensnare you they will, unless you have the necessary power of resistance which the very fact of reading these words indicates you have not.

Undoubtedly you will already possess one or two tools, even though they have remained neglected for years, or have been applied in operations they were never designed for but for which they were possibly better suited. But others will appear as and when their need arises, not that there will be any connection, stated or implied, between the acquisition of any of them and the carefully camouflaged task ahead.

Strangely enough there seems to be a marked opposition on the part of a wife towards her husband borrowing any tools he may require from a neighbour or friend. She, herself, will borrow with impunity groceries, knitting patterns, books, gramophone records, umbrellas, bus fares, jewellery and even clothes, but if her husband suggests borrowing a tenon saw from 'next door' there is a distinct drop in the temperature.

This has nothing to do with moral considerations. She is in no way concerned with the possibility of the article's return being overlooked, or that it may be done a mischief while in her husband's custody, or that it may result in retaliatory borrowing. It is just that she has no wish for it to be known that her husband is not properly equipped. And this mysterious feminine pride in the possession of a handyman must not be jeopardised by the slightest hint of inadequacy in either equipment or ability. In fact, if he would but realise it, his *image* as a handyman is vastly more important than all the creations, conversions or innovations which he might achieve or attempt to achieve. You may have noticed that a wife seldom *displays* the wonders he has worked – she only tells about them. It is the *man* that matters.

If only he could believe this, what a wonderfully unassailable position he would find himself in. All the trump cards are in his hand – if only he would dare to play them. But there always remains that canker of un-certainty – it might just not be true in his case and to test it might be fatal. This is the snag and, of course, the final trump in his wife's hand.

That is not to say that the various projects she launches him on are merely superfluous. Some of them fill very real needs in her domestic plans. It is the quality of the work which is unimportant – up to a point, at least.

54

'She will borrow with impunity'

Her account of it to her friends will always be glowing, and should they in an unguarded moment chance upon a sample, she will be ready with explanations to justify gaping joints, leaking seams or peeling polish.

But to get back to the point, this does not mean that there will be no borrowing. Far from it. Only that it will be done with discrimination. Borrowing will usually be restricted to tools for which you have only a limited use, and tools which are expensive.

Most households possess a hammer, a screwdriver and

a saw, together with a few assorted nails, some slightly bent and most slightly rusty, and some mixed screws, burred and paint-encrusted. These seem to be the basic equipment for married life once the honeymoon is over. And although much can be accomplished with these simple implements, one day a job will come along which is quite beyond their modest scope and at least one more piece of equipment is deemed to be necessary. So you buy it or it is bought for you, depending on the urgency of the job and who is coming to stay.

Another day, another job, another tool. And so gradually the tool-kit grows and grows, bringing with it the problem of their accommodation – and still you never have quite the right tool for the next job. You may make do with what you have but there is always the gnawing feeling of inadequacy. But against this should be set the satisfaction of having a ready-made excuse for a botched-up job.

Still, however many tools you have, be they few or many, they must be kept somewhere, preferably where you will know where to find them when required.

You may commence, as many do at first, by popping them in the drawer of the kitchen-table with the other cutting and hole-making instruments like knives and forks. But even if there is no protest, and that would be strange, it is simply asking for them to be misused by the only other member of the family likely to use that drawer.

It may not be their misuse which will concern you – a little competition in this may even be healthy – it is more likely to be the fact that they will be left at the scene of their most recent crime and not returned to the place where you should expect to find them. Nothing is more irritating or more conducive to the postponement of a task than failure to locate the tools you need to perform it.

And it's no use asking who had them last. There never was such a silence as follows that question. Usually you need to be either a Sherlock Holmes or a clairvoyant to discover their hiding-place before your interest in the job cools off.

Mind, circumstances may be very different if the job is an urgent one your wife wants carried out. In that case simply announce that you are unable to do it as the tools have disappeared, and sit back. You will not relax for long. The tools will appear as though by magic.

However, there must come a time when the competition between your tools and her kitchen utensils for space in the drawer can no longer be ignored. You do not need to ask which will win. So you progress to a tool-box.

This may be a simple thing with a bottom and four sides, or an elaborate affair with fittings, partitions, clips, drawers and a lockable lid.

You will probably commence with the open box, and the tools will be placed inside in a reasonably untidy pile. As the tools increase the box becomes heavier so that eventually the box is not taken to the site of the job but the tools are taken from the box where it lies. This is usually a fairly inaccessible and gloomy corner, not necessarily chosen by you but proved beyond arguable doubt to be the only possible place for it in view of all the other more urgent demands on available space.

This being so, bear in mind the difficulty of selecting

57

the tool you want, and the tendency for chisels and saws to lie with their armaments uppermost, and keep the first-aid kit as near to the tool-box as possible.

As you become more skilled in the use of the tools, or as the period of your possession of them lengthens and you *feel* you are more skilled (whichever is the more obvious), you may also become more concerned for their welfare. In consequence you will observe that keen-edged tools like chisels lose much of their keenness by being tossed nonchalantly into the box at the end of any operation. You will accordingly place them in the box more carefully, which is a step in the approved direction.

'*saws . . . with their armaments uppermost*'

But even jostling them about as you fumble for a screwdriver or a hammer is bad for their well-being. You may compromise by wrapping the business end in several thicknesses of newspaper, but in time you will become restless for a more efficient layout. This is when you progress to a fitted tool-box.

In this such items as chisels, bits, saws etc. are held firm against the lid or base of the box in clips, and if returned there after use you will always know where to find them.

The only problem is that others will also know where to find them – and without the risk of a lacerated finger! This is where the lockable lid comes in – and possibly where the marriage ends. So you must decide for yourself which it is more important for you to keep intact – your wife or your tools.

'the marriage ends'

Three

Working Space

Let us assume that you now have your kit of tools and the wherewithal to protect them. The next question is – where do you work?

This will sometimes be decided by the location of the job itself, but if there is any preparatory work to be done you will need somewhere to do it.

Unless you have a wife who doesn't mind sawdust and shavings on the lounge carpet, and few don't, the usual starting point is the kitchen.

This is quite satisfactory provided you choose a time when your wife will not be using the kitchen during the progress of your work, so that you can spread yourself without fear of protest, either spoken or sniffed. There is only one drawback – there is no such time!

You may seek assurance beforehand that access to the kitchen will not be required for the next hour, and you may even jeopardise conjugal bliss by repeating the request in different words to be doubly sure. You may even receive the assurance and accept it in all good faith. But you'll be wrong. Oh, yes. You'll be wrong.

Just as soon as you have the various parts of your work carefully assembled, maybe even freshly glued, or when you are in a precarious position yourself with your sharpest chisel dangerously poised, or with your piping hot soldering-iron a fraction of an uncomfortable inch from the tips of your fingers – without warning the door will burst open and even as the cry of exquisite anguish leaves your lips you will remember my words.

Nor will it do any good to quote her recently given assurance. By ancient tradition the kitchen has always been the woman's domain in which the presence of man is only ever tolerated – even when washing-up. And when a woman wants something from the kitchen, or to do something in it, the want is immediate and brooks no delay. So pipe down!

You could, of course, barricade the door with the refrigerator or stick a wedge underneath it unless you are, by nature, a man of peace. Much better find an alternative working space as soon as possible.

Your next choice will probably be the garage if you have one. If you haven't you can skip this section.

Much will depend on the size of the garage and whether you will have room to work if you share the garage with a car. This problem will vary from time to time according to the size of the job on hand.

In any case you will need a working surface, which will indicate the need for a work-bench. Now you are becoming more professional. Your next decision – do you buy one or make one? The answer depends on how substantial you want it to be.

Your decision may, in fact, be made easier by the next question arising. How do you make a work-bench when you haven't a work-bench on which to make it? Undoubtedly, in the long run, it is more prudent to buy one than to spend much of your time reinforcing a home-made one – and less embarrassing.

Before having an ambitious bench delivered, ensure that there is room in the garage for both bench and car, even if there is insufficient room to work as well. But to have to move the bench into the drive when you want to garage the car, or leave the car out all night to protect your bench, while not impracticable in the summer can be tedious in the winter, and remember that the latter is the longer by about 350 days.

Provided there is room to house both at the same time the car can, of course, be temporarily evicted while the bench is in use. That way it is less likely to suffer the indignities of dents and abrasions from tools wielded with more enthusiasm than expertise. Even so, if access to the garage is direct from the house, or if your wife also drives the car, it might be better to have second thoughts about setting up your workshop there. This is more a matter of diplomacy than prejudice, and after all the garage is no longer a male preserve, if, indeed, it ever was.

By far the best solution, if space and money allow, is to erect a workshop completely separate from the house – if possible at the far end of the garden beyond the carrying limits of the human voice. You can either make it yourself or buy it in sections ready for erecting. If you purchase a sectional shed you will need another pair of hands to assist in its assembly, so prepare for this emergency by being nice to the body designate well before the arrival date of the shed.

One word of warning – you will find that there is only just enough of everything to complete the shed, so that if one section seems to be a little too full along the seams somewhere and you decide to reduce its size with a saw,

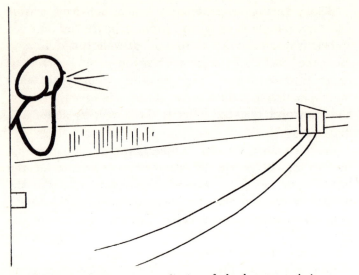

'beyond the carrying limits of the human voice'

resist the temptation as you would another 'one for the road', because it will undoubtedly prove that you had the wrong section, or it was upside-down or inside-out, and once cut you will ever after have a permanent draught, not to mention an automatic sprinkler system when it rains.

Once erected, felted and creosoted you can now set about purchasing a bench to fit it, and fix up racks for all your tools so that everything is visible and to hand when wanted. If you are near enough to the house to run an electric cable you can also have electric light, heat and kettle. If you are too far away, or have a healthy respect for electricity, you can resort to calor gas, or invest in a paraffin lamp and heater, and a fire extinguisher.

With a carefully appointed and well-equipped shed you may now think you are ready to enjoy many hours of happy monastic leisure. What an innocent you are!

You remember that old bicycle of your wife's with the two flat tyres and the rust-encrusted frame you used to bark your shins on every time you went into the garage? It isn't there any more, is it? Remember that roll of linoleum intended for the kitchen but which was superseded by lino tiles like those Mrs Carstairs has, before ever it could be used? It used to take up quite a bit of space in the spare room, didn't it? But it doesn't any more. Those big pictures with the heavy oak frames your mother gave you when you were married, that used to be in the cupboard under the stairs. Have you noticed how much more room there is now – or was, until it became occupied by the new shopping trolley?

What has happened to all these things, not to mention the pair of steps with the split tread, the ironing-board with the broken hinge, the curtain poles which were replaced by rails, the old vacuum cleaner and the bureau with acute woodworm? Where are they all?

Wait until you go down to your shed again!

So you are back to the kitchen once more. But there is another snag now that you didn't have before. Your tools are at the bottom of the garden.

But as far as your wife is concerned you *have* a workshop, and she can (and will) mention that you have one. And so you will probably be the means of other husbands having workshops they cannot use.

But if you, or they, think that this is going to give you an excuse for not doing all the jobs you didn't want to do in the shed anyway – don't deceive yourselves. You'll just have to make do as you did before you had the shed, and if you are lucky you may even be allowed to pop one or two redundant articles of your own in it from time to time, but don't rely on it.

'Your tools are at the bottom of the garden'

Four

Getting on with the Job

Ready or not, you must eventually arrive at the point when procrastination is no longer possible. A challenge will be thrown down in such terms that you cannot possibly ignore it, or pretend not to understand it, without betraying what remains of your manhood.

If you are fortunate it will be a job you have seen someone else do, or read about in a book, or even one which has no technical complications but merely requires the application of a little common sense. If so, you are lucky indeed.

On the other hand it may be one of infinite difficulty, requiring experience, skill, inexhaustible patience, dozens of extra tools and the assistance of craftsmen.

But, whichever it is, be assured that you will not sleep easy, if you are allowed to sleep at all, until you have grappled with the problem.

Now whatever job you tackle, under whatever circumstances, the second time you face it is much easier than the first. You have all the mistakes of the first experience behind you and only the new mistakes to worry about. To give you an advantage over all other *new* handymen, and to enable you to start at the second stage instead of the first, the following pages contain what would have been your experience on confronting certain fairly common tasks for the first time.

'You have all the mistakes behind you'

This should get a lot of basic blunders out of your system without your ever having waved a saw in anger.

The normal text-book always seems to assume a certain knowledge on the part of the reader. This book, at the risk of being over-optimistic, assumes nothing. And although some of the problems envisaged may never arise, there is no earthly reason why they shouldn't.

Please don't think that the problems dealt with are imaginary. They are either the direct result of painful personal experience or have been gleaned from other battle-scarred veterans over the rare, commiserative half-pint at the local.

Now *there's* a place to gain valuable information – if only your domestic preoccupations would allow the time. Whatever problem you are tangled up with someone there has always been enmeshed in it before, and found the way out, and you will always find them willing, even anxious, to pass on the benefit of their experience.

But be cautious about accepting such advice from a 'regular'. If he was as experienced as he suggests he would not have time to be a regular.

Once having committed yourself to a particular job the great thing is to approach it confidently. It may well be said that success depends on that one word – *confidence*.

Let no hint of indecision creep into your actions, whether marking out the work, sorting the tools, or merely surveying the scene of your approaching conflict. It sometimes helps to indulge in a little whistling or humming, or you might even burst right out into song, provided the tune is gay and the words are not foreboding.

You won't be kidding anyone – not even yourself – and it won't last long, but it feels good while it does.

It is not, of course, possible to cover every eventuality in a book like this. It would only spread depression if it were. What has been omitted must be filled in by experience. After all, we are told that experience is the greatest teacher – if not always the speediest or the most comfortable.

So, to work. . . .

Five

A Dripping Tap

Let us commence with something simple yet quite inevitable. A dripping tap. Everyone says it's simple, especially those who have never tried to cure it. No one needs to say it's inevitable; it speaks for itself.

One thing is certain – a dripping tap cannot be ignored. Something *has* to be done about it. Anyone who has ever sat for any length of time in the same room as one will confirm that there is no quicker way to a state of mental distress than by way of the steady drip, drip, drip, of water. It is not the volume of noise it makes – goodness knows it's quiet enough – but it's the steady insistence that does the damage.

Of course, it could be argued that not many people sit in a room where there is a tap, much less a *dripping* tap, but the discomfort applies even more if you are kneeling down, standing up or pacing back and fore.

It is all right until you notice it. You can be in its presence for hours or even days without being aware of it, like the ticking clock you look at frequently but never hear. But once you notice that drip, or some sadistic person draws your attention to it by an unkind or irritable comment, you are done. You could have a brass-band playing at full blast in the same room and you would still hear that drip above the thump of the big drum and the oompah of the tuba.

'a state of mental distress'

Anyway, let us assume that the dripping tap has been brought to your notice either by the drip itself or by the complaints from the usual source, and that the need for its repair has not only been suggested but even forcefully stated.

It is strange that everyone seems to know that when a tap develops a drip it is because the washer is worn. This knowledge is possessed by people who have never seen a washer and who would not recognise one if they did, and yet the information is imparted with the supreme confidence of one teethed on leaking taps.

You, of course, are included among those experts and you approach your task confident in the knowledge that it is the washer which requires renewing and nothing else. In ninety-nine cases out of a hundred this is correct, too. Strange, isn't it?

So what do you do?

From your tool box, cupboard, shed or what have you, you obtain a spanner, wrench, pliers, or anything which is suitable for undoing the nut on the tap which holds everything together.

(Unfortunately the spanner, wrench and pliers were not mentioned among the tools dealt with earlier, but when the chapter was written the tap had not begun to drip. But, in brief, these particular tools have the effect of adding a handle to a nut to make it easier to turn.)

Sometimes you find that you cannot see the nut although you know it's there somewhere. This is because the manufacturers who do not like amateurs messing around with their products have concealed it beneath a metal hood. Don't be put off by this. By turning the hood in an anti-clockwise direction (if it will budge at all) it will unscrew and you can slide it up the spindle. Unfortunately it will not stay there and you will have to hold it with one hand while continuing your work with the other.

For the purpose of this exercise I am assuming that the hood on your tap (if it has a hood) is one that will allow itself to be unscrewed. If it won't, you have another problem on your hands which we will by-pass for the

73

moment, if not altogether.

Raising the hood exposes the nut which you need to undo before proceeding. So you apply your spanner or wrench to the nut and turn firmly towards the wall – the nut, of course, not you. Continue until the whole assembly is released. You will know when this is, because a jet of water will hit the ceiling and cascade over everyone and everything in sight.

This will serve to remind you that before monkeying about with taps you should turn the water off at the main.

Now, do you know the situation of the stopcock, which is the name given to the tap which controls the main water supply? If you don't you're in dead trouble because one thing is certain, you've got to find out. And while you are doing this the water, which is rapidly turning your kitchen into an aquarium, will refuse to be discouraged by any attempt to reinsert the tap.

The stopcock is usually situated somewhere between the front door and the road, or it may be at the back of the house. Difficult, isn't it?

It may be somewhere beneath the tarmac you had laid on the drive last year, or beneath the birdbath your wife had cemented to the patio to cover up the square of metal which looked so unsightly.

By this time it is probably raining as though it had only just heard of Noah, so before going out and getting wetter still, check whether there is a tap inside the house which controls the main flow. If so it is well beneath the surface of the water by now but you should be able to locate it with a few deep breaths.

'turning your kitchen into an aquarium'

Whichever tap you discover, when you turn it you will probably find that nothing happens at all. This is because the water you are wading through is coming to you by courtesy of a large tank in the loft and will continue to do so until the tank is empty. This is therefore a good time to put on the kettle and make a pot of tea while there is still water available and before it reaches the gas-jets. It may be some time before refreshments are again possible.

While you are waiting for the tank to empty you can examine the tap assembly and check whether everyone's opinion has been confirmed and the washer really does need renewing. If it does you feel relieved. If it doesn't you just feel wet.

Supposing you find the washer needs to be renewed. You now have a nerve-shattering thought. You don't have a spare washer. It's also early-closing day, and even if it wasn't you don't have a boat.

It's going to be a long night. It only remains for you to make it up with your wife, and if you think that is possible just wait until you really have a leaking tap.

Sorry to leave you in this predicament, but at least a number of mistakes have been covered which you do not need to make again. And anyway, it's high time you got out of those wet things or you won't be here to finish reading this book.

Six

Making a Bookshelf

It is not surprising if, after acquiring a kit of wood-working tools, however modest, you feel an urge to use them, or at least some of them. On the other hand it would still not be surprising if you hated the very sight of them and occupied your spare time thinking out ways and means of *not* using them, or even of disposing of them.

But, bearing in mind what has already been said, even if you develop a deep disaffection for them this will not deter someone from ensuring that they are not allowed to remain idle very long. So take the bull by the horns, and the tool-box by surprise, and get acquainted with its contents (the tool-box's not the bull's) by carrying out some simple operation – like putting up a bookshelf.

You may not need a bookshelf but don't let that stop you. Once you have erected the shelf you might buy a book and then you will have somewhere to put it. This might even be the beginning of something bigger than both of you. One book leading to another, and another, and then a second bookshelf . . . .

But we digress. We haven't erected the first one yet.

The best position for your first shelf will be in the recess beside the fireplace. This will provide you with ready-made ends for the books to lean on should they not be big enough to stand up for themselves. The side walls are also more convenient for fixing the shelf supports to. The alternative would be to use a pair of brackets which are more unsightly, especially since they rarely permit themselves to be fixed at the same heights or in a truly vertical position.

So let it be the recess. Your first job is to fix the supports for the shelf to rest on. These should be screwed one on the side of the chimney-breast and the other on the opposite wall so that they are facing each other.

For the supports obtain pieces of $1\frac{1}{2}'' \times \frac{3}{4}''$ or $1\frac{1}{2}'' \times 1''$, or anything similar. You will need two pieces as long as the width of the shelf. If you haven't bought the wood for the shelf yet bear in mind that you do not want it any wider than the depth of the recess at the chimney-breast end or it will be jutting out into the room, and the home is already the place where most accidents happen, they say. For the same reason let the size of both supports be dictated by the depth of the chimney-breast rather than the size of the opposite wall.

To fix the supports you will first need to 'plug' the wall. In the old days this meant knocking a large hole in the wall which was then filled with a piece of wood into which the support was nailed. The modern method is to use an electric drill to make the hole which, while starting off quite small, frequently changes into a gaping wound from which the flow of plaster is now staunched with an asbestos compound moistened with water, instead of a wooden plug. Into this compound the supports should be screwed *not* nailed, which takes longer, is more tiring, and is up to you.

It is advisable to prepare the supports by drilling holes

'your books are going to be in a bit of a mess'

through them to ease the passage of the screws until they meet the wall. These holes should not be of greater diameter than the heads of the screws for reasons which will become obvious if you fail to heed the warning.

79

Two screws should be sufficient for each support provided they are at opposite ends. And don't forget that the screws should be long enough, not only to go through the wood, but as far into the wall as prudence and your drilling will permit.

Now you have fixed both supports step back and take a careful look at them. Do you notice something? The one is a good six inches lower than the other, isn't it? Which means your books are going to be in a bit of a mess.

What you should have done, of course, is to measure the required position of each support from the picture rail so that they end up exactly opposite each other. In the absence of a picture rail, measure from where the picture rail would have been.

Now you have to decide whether to lower the high one or raise the low one, and this is purely a matter of personal taste.

If raising the lower one means the shelf is going to be too high you can always use it for the books you intend to buy and not read. But whether you decide to raise or lower you are going to be left with two unsightly screw-holes and you can't raise or lower these.

Let us assume, however, that the problem has been resolved and the two supports are in their final resting-place, and that no one is wishing that anyone else was. Next comes the shelf or, rather, you have to go and get it. It will probably be a piece of wood something like 9′ wide and $\frac{3}{4}′$ thick and a bit longer than you need so that you can cut it to the exact size. While the width and thickness can vary according to personal preference, the

'It fell straight through'

length should always be the same.

Next, measure carefully the distance between the two supports. Having measured once, measure again. Carpenters have an excellent motto which says 'Measure twice and cut once'. When you come to think of it it would be impossible to reverse the procedure.

Right. Now mark off the measurements along your piece of shelving and with your square make a pencil mark right across the surface of the wood. This is your sawing guide. If you are in doubt about your measurement now is the time to check – not after you have sawn. Now saw.

Your shelf will now sit snugly on top of the supports and the job is almost complete. Well, it should have sat snugly. But it didn't, did it? It fell straight through, didn't it? You know why? When you measured the distance between the supports you should have measured the distance between the further edges not the nearer ones.

So now you have one piece of useless shelving and two supports supporting nothing. If you are not disheartened by this and in spite of everything you still feel you want a shelf, or, to put it another way, if your wife is still tapping her toe, it's another trip to the do-it-yourself shop to get another piece of timber. But at least you won't make the same mistake again, will you?

Want to bet?

Let us suppose you have persevered with the shelf and it is now complete. Well, complete as far as the carpentry is concerned. You can't leave it in the bare wood, can you? Well, you might be able to but you won't be allowed to. So you have to decide how you are going to 'finish it off'.

There are various possibilities, such as veneering, staining and varnishing, staining and French polishing, or painting.

Which you choose doesn't matter very much. What does matter is that you have left it a bit late – for the supports, anyway. To apply any of these finishes now is going to mean messing up the wall. You should have thought of it before the final fixing.

You can ignore these words if you wish and proceed with the final rites, but be in no doubt the light will always fall strongest on the stain or paint smudges that, whatever pains you take, will find their way on to the otherwise unblemished wall.

The alternative is to take the shelf and supports down again, prepare them carefully with sandpaper and apply whatever finish you prefer before returning them to the wall.

There is now only one drawback. Every time the screwdriver slips off the head of the screw-head now it will leave an angry weal on the polished surface that no amount of 'touching-up' will ever completely eradicate.

Still, you've got your shelf.

Seven

Modernising Doors

If you now have ordinary panelled doors, sooner or later your wife will express the wish they were flush doors like Cynthia's, with no ledges to collect dust, and not so old-fashioned looking. From an innocent remark (unless you are already learning to recognise the symptoms) this will grow through the days into a matter of such urgency that you will begin to wonder how the country has existed this far with all the old type of doors it must contain.

So, in the interest of peace, and because you recognise the inevitability, you agree to convert them all to flush doors. After all, it's simple enough. It only means putting a sheet of hardboard on either side.

Oh, man, when will you learn!

Never mind, let's start on one door. Pick any one you wish. The kitchen door? Because it's the least important and any mistakes won't matter? Whatever you say.

First of all you measure the door so that you can buy the necessary hardboard. You have already learned your lesson about measuring so you measure again and again, put your various answers down and take an average.

Armed with your measurements you go to the do-it-yourself shop and purchase the hardboard. They are beginning to know you now. You have been back so often to buy the same things. Not that they know why.

They are only guessing.

You hand in your measurements, they cut the sheets to size, they hand them over and you pay for them. Now your troubles start.

You didn't bring the car because you knew you couldn't get the hardboard inside. Instead, you came by bus. But you can't go home by bus. The conductor has enough problems already without having half his bus partitioned off. So you have to walk. It isn't too far. You've done it before, even with a couple of shopping bags, when the car broke down. So with a brave smile at the manager you pick up the sheets of hardboard and step out of the shop.

You had forgotten about the wind outside, hadn't you? The hardboard, acting like a most effective sail, carries you forcibly into the pavement stall of the greengrocer next door, sending fruit and vegetables in all directions. It's embarrassing enough picking up the scattered produce to the accompaniment of the greengrocer's invective without, at the same time, trying to protect your door panels from the hurrying feet of pedestrians with no time to stop and help.

Finally, the last sprout and artichoke are back on the stall, the greengrocer has pocketed your proffered 50p and you are ready to sail on your way. There's no point in recounting all the incidents which punctuate your progress along the High Street and back to Acacia Drive. You will be able to read it in the faces of your neighbours for days to come. What matters now is that your wife still wants flush doors.

If it hasn't occurred to you that fastening a large hardboard panel on to a door while it is still hanging in its familiar position is difficult, an unhappy experience lies ahead. Whatever method of fixing you select, to hold a heavy, unwieldly panel in position requires all of two hands, while the fixing requires at least another two, and they should all, preferably, belong to the same body since each pair should know instinctively what the other two are up to. If you are made that way, good for you, but if not the best thing to do is to take the door off its hinges and lay it down on a firm surface.

Taking the door down is simple enough. All you have to do is unscrew the screws fastening it to the hinges. When the last one is removed, or sometimes even before, there is a sudden lurch on the part of the door as it and the doorframe part company, unless you have miscounted the screws and the doorframe comes away as well. But, with or without the frame, doors are suprisingly heavy as you will note while crawling from under it.

Place the top end of the door on the seat of one chair and the foot on the seat of another and you have the door in a reclining position – *prone* if the door opens inwards and *supine* if it opens outwards. It is also at a more convenient height for working than if placed on the floor.

Before going any further, check the measurements again to be sure the panel really does fit the door. Or if over the years the door has lost a little bit of height here or a little bit of width there, as doors will, now is the time to make the necessary adjustments with saw or plane – but to the panel not the door.

The best way of securing the panel to the door is undoubtedly by impact glue. This is a glue applied to

87

both surfaces and when they meet after drying they are united for ever more. So you will appreciate the importance of precision in your movements.

The glue is usually supplied in a tin together with the tooth-edged implement necessary to spread the thick fluid which has an obstinate tendency when poured from the tin to stay in one spot.

So you spread the glue as evenly as possible over the panel, particularly where it comes into contact with the raised parts of the door. While this is drying spread a thin layer of the glue over the surface of the door. There is no point in gluing the small panels of the door as the hardboard will never make contact with them – not unless someone kicks it in.

When both are dry they are brought into contact with each other. And this is where great care must be taken to ensure a perfect fit. So first, nail a strip of wood along one edge of the door so that it projects above the surface. The panel can then be 'trued-up' against this before lowering

'You've forgotten to remove the handles'

it on to the door.

It isn't until you hold the panel over the door, preparing to lower it into position, that you realise just how wayward a large sheet of hardboard can be. It wobbles like a jelly and you cannot be blamed if you panic. But carry on. Lower one edge steadily against the guide. Right. Now slowly down with the whole sheet on to the door.

All goes well until you come to the opposite side and you find it refuses to lie flat. Know what you've done? Yes, you've forgotten to remove the door handles!

It's too bad but that's one panel that can be written off. Even if you remove the handles now the panel has already joined up with the door in all the wrong places and will never be the same again. Nothing remains but to remove the panel and restart from the beginning.

In removing the panel you realise just how good the glue is. So much of the panel refuses to be parted from the door and large patches of hardboard remain behind giving the door a piebald appearance. Getting these patches off is no fun but you certainly can't leave them there, so get on with it.

Now you need another panel. The man at the do-it-yourself shop is going to love you, but look out for the greengrocer. He may have a good memory.

When you are ready to begin again, check the measurements as before and make any adjustments necessary. Spread the glue as before and try and keep it off the carpet this time.

You have the guide strip already nailed to the edge of the door and you know the drill from here on. Line the panel up against the strip and gently lower on to the door. This time it lies completely flat and only requires a little pressure exerted over the whole area to make a perfect bond, but a few panel pins can be driven in around the edges – just in case. These should be punched well into the hardboard and the holes filled with a plastic filler so that your lack of faith remains unrevealed once the door has been painted.

You now turn the door over and panel the other side in exactly the same way, but leaving out the first stage. After all, if you have removed one handle you should have removed both.

That leaves you with a very expensive-looking door, and in this case its looks do not belie it. The next job is to replace the handles.

But where?

You really should have thought of that before fixing the second panel. It would have been so easy to bore a hole in the hardboard through the hole already in the door. Now it's going to be a matter of trial and error unless you are rash enough to take one of the panels off again. You may be lucky, of course, and find the right spot after only four or five attempts. But just in case, bore the trial holes in a neat pattern so that if the worst comes to the worst you can pretend the holes were intentional.

Finally, you have to rehang the door. You may think this sounds quite an easy job, but you are probably already beginning to learn that nothing is quite as easy as it seems, and rehanging the door is no exception.

First of all you will notice that with a panel on either side the door feels five times as heavy as when you took it down. And whereas a door will practically come down on its own with just a little judicious help to the screws, you will find that nothing will prompt it to jump back again. This is where you could really do with some help.

If you and your wife are still on speaking terms, in spite of the glue on the carpet and the torn wallpaper when the door fell down, you could do worse than seek her assistance in holding the door steady for you.

Your problem is the gap between the door and the floor. If it wasn't there it would be easy. So what you want is something the same size to rest it on – the door, that is. And believe it or believe it not, of all the pieces of wood you have been storing in the shed 'in case they should come in handy', not one of them will be the right thickness. So you must make do with the nearest you have, coupled with a little grunting, a lot of breath-holding and face-reddening, and the ability to ignore the pointed remarks from the other side of the door.

When you can jockey the hinge into its recess and drive home just one screw the battle is nearly over. Get the other screws in as quickly as possible before anything else can go amiss. When the last screw is given its final turn, stand back and admire your new door and receive with all modesty your wife's well-merited praise.

Now try and close the door!

It won't, will it? In fact you can almost feel the strain on the hinges as you try to force it. Don't force it too much unless you want to start all over again. The trouble is the doorstop – that strip of wood around the doorframe that prevents the door from going right through into the breakfast room. The door now being thicker than it was is meeting the doorstop much sooner than it was meant to, so it will need to be moved back the thickness of the hardboard.

This shouldn't take long unless you happen to break the doorstop while taking it off, and then, apart from the painting, the job is complete.

How many doors did you say there were to be done? Seven? Ah well!

Eight

Papering a Room

This is the kind of job which, having completed it satisfactorily once, you will find lying in wait for you at the first signs of spring every year for the rest of your days.

It's a sobering thought, so think it over carefully before committing yourself. If you decide to proceed, read on.

Once it has been determined which room is to be papered you will be kept in a state of hypertension for days while the paper is being chosen.

You will be cajoled or harassed into visiting the wallpaper shop where hours will be spent pouring over pattern books – books you have elbowed your way to through dithering groups of would-be decorators.

Your eyes will follow the slowly turning patterns of flowers and leaves and stripes and squiggles in grotesque colours until your brain feels like a frustrated kaleidoscope.

To punctuations of *oohs* and *ahs,* approved patterns will be acclaimed and then abandoned for even more favourable ones. These in turn will be lost among the capricious pages of the book so that substitutes have to be found and considered with as much painstaking care as the originals. The fact that at least three couples are now queueing for access to the book you have been hogging so long, embarrasses no one but you.

'hours will be spent pouring over pattern books'

When you believe a final choice has been made at last, and you are about to call the assistant to take your order, a violent nudge in your ribs reduces you to painful silence, broken only by a soft tearing sound as a piece is surreptitiously detached from the pattern 'to see if it goes with the curtains and carpet'.

This means further visits to the shop until at last a final desperate decision is reached and only the ordering remains.

Do you know how many pieces you require? It will depend not only on the size of the room but on its height, too, and also the pattern of the paper since some are more wasteful than others when it comes to matching. And if you think you can get away without matching you are a greater optimist than anyone deserves to be.

The best thing is to measure the room carefully, leaving out doors, windows and fitted furniture and give the details to the shop assistant. He will tell you how many pieces you *should* need, then add one more. This will compensate for those pieces you cut too short, drop on the floor paste-side down, put your foot through or put on and take off the wall so many times you daren't risk it again.

The assistant will also be able to tell you how much cold water paste you need, and here, too, it is better to purchase an extra packet as buckets of paste are prone to tip or be stepped into.

In addition, if you do not already possess them or know who does, you should buy a paste-brush and a paper-hanging brush. Buckets, scissors, pencils, dusters, floorclothes and drawing-pins will usually be found around the house if you know where to look.

Before commencing work it is advisable to remove curtains, carpets, furniture and all family pets, then whiten the windows so that the neighbours are unable to enjoy your misery.

The first stage is the removal of the old paper or papers from the walls. This is done by soaking it well with water applied with the paste-brush. Allow a little time for the water to soak well into the paper and floorboards before proceeding. Then scrape off the paper with a scraper which you should also have bought with the brushes. This is a very tiring job but is frequently made more difficult by allowing insufficient time for the water to soak in, or waiting too long so that it dries out.

When the scraping is complete you should have an

'the removal of the old paper'

expanse of naked wall and a pile of wet paper clinging in ever-increasing garlands to your feet. You should also have a fair sized blister in the middle of your palm.

If you haven't already mixed the paste, do this next. The instructions are detailed on the packet and there is no problem except that had you done it before the scraping the blister would not be so painful.

The only article of furniture remaining in the room should be a table and on this you will paste the paper.

First, to cut the paper into lengths. The initial piece is easy because you don't have to match anything. But make sure it is a little longer than you need so that you can trim off the top and the bottom which never seem to get pasted anyway.

The second and subsequent pieces can be cut by matching the pattern against the first – before it is stuck on the wall. But don't cut too many full-length pieces as you are bound to need some short ones – unless your room lacks a fireplace and window.

You are now ready to begin pasting. Place the pieces of paper on the table so that they overlap each other to take up the overflow of paste from the first piece. Now dip the paste brush in the paste and *slap* the paste on to the paper as though trying to paste the piece underneath. This is supposed to assist the penetration of the paste – the splashing of the wall is purely incidental.

By the way, you *are* pasting the *back* or *unpatterned* side of the paper, aren't you? If not you can write that piece off and start again.

As you paste one half of the piece fold the paper over and slide the whole to one side to enable you to complete

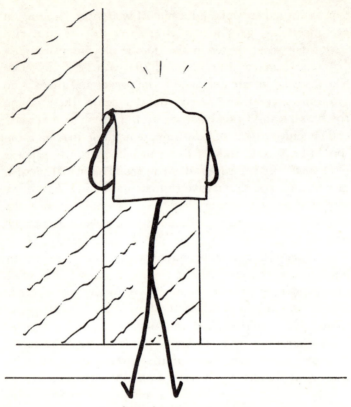

'curling down to meet you'

the other half. When pasted fold that over too. You should now be ready to approach the wall.

This is the point at which the nerve visibly wilts. This is the moment of truth – it only *seems* like an hour.

Having lifted the piece from the table try not to dither too long. After all, the paste is only paste and there is a limit to its endurance.

Also, any delay may result in your folds unfolding, in which case you will find your path to the wall carpeted with the paper which should be adorning it.

But let us suppose that you have reached the wall without mishap . . .

It is recommended that you begin at the side of the window and work towards the door. This enables you to face away from the window and be less conspicuous.

At this stage a small pair of steps are useful although a stool or wooden box may serve equally well to give you that little extra height necessary to line up the paper.

Hold the paper an inch or two from the wall and swing it gently sideways until it reaches a position parallel with the wall and in line with the edge of the window, then advance smartly until the paper and wall make contact. Place one hand firmly in the middle of the paper and smooth outwards in all directions. This movement should be repeated with the paper-hanging brush until the whole of the paper is adhering to the wall.

This, at least, is the theory. In practice, when you get about halfway down, you will find the top half curling down to meet you and unless you notice it in time your hair will wipe most of the paste off the back of the paper.

Push it back quickly, brushing right, left and centre at panic speed while there is still some active paste remaining on the wall. Then, with one hand holding the top half firmly against the wall brush the lower half thoroughly into position. If the paper should remain in contact with the wall, mark with the point of your scissors where the paper meets the picture rail and then ease the paper away from the wall and trim along the crease. When this is done try to brush the paper back against the wall. You may think this is asking too much so, if necessary, apply a little additional paste to the wall, but there is no need to mention this to anyone.

You will need to carry out the same trimming operation where the paper meets the skirting. But this time you will find it much easier unless you are still standing on the steps.

Now stand back and view what you have done. If you notice a number of air bubbles under the paper, some larger than others, don't be surprised. It nearly always happens. You can try to brush or squeeze them out if you like or take your glasses off and pretend they are not there.

Some of these bubbles will dry out in time and others will collapse from sheer exhaustion, while others will remain to gloat for ever.

Repeat the process with each subsequent piece, remembering to match the pattern each time, until you come to the door. You will probably find that you only need a fraction of the width of the paper to complete the wall. It always happens like that although it would not require much ingenuity on the part of builders to make their walls of a size equally divisible by the width of wallpapers. But they don't, so measure the size you require and mark it off on the next piece and cut with the scissors.

Don't assume, though, that the width you need will be the same at the top as at the bottom. Neither the wall nor

'Have you noticed your feet lately?'

the doorframe, not to mention your paperhanging, is as accurate as that. So cut your piece accordingly.

You have probably heard the old music-hall joke about the man who, ignoring the windows and door, continued papering and was unable to find his way out of the room. In practice this will be impossible as your wife will keep coming in and out to see how you are getting on so that the door will be open almost as much as it is closed, and not even with the best paper in the world can you hang paper in an open space.

This continual traffic makes the doorway a dangerous place to linger and you will be relieved to leave it for a while and recommence operations on the other side of the window, working your way past the chimney-breast until you reach the door from the other side. By this time your paste-bucket will be fairly empty and not quite so accident prone.

By the way, have you noticed your feet lately? They look as though you are wearing snowshoes, don't they? These are waste ends you have been cutting from the tops and bottoms of pieces already on the wall. They always fall paste-side up and adhere to your shoes.

Before it is too late, remove them and store them in a place of safety in the centre of the room, and see that all future offcuts are similarly safeguarded. This is not a matter of tidiness but of expediency. You may need them.

You see, you always leave the wall under the window till last since it only needs short pieces. Also, being away from the light (at least during daylight hours), pattern matching is not so vital. Now if you have been unlucky and have miscalculated your needs, or had the misfortune to put the brush or fingers through the centre of too many pieces, or been a little abandoned with the scissors, you may need even those grubby offcuts to complete the room. In fact, you may even be chasing your wife to salvage the pieces she has taken out on her feet. It *has* happened.

By the way, you can safely ignore any picture nails in the wall. They are usually stronger than the paper and will tear their way through and can be used again. The paper will settle down around the base of the nail as though nothing had ever happened.

With all the paper safely on the wall – well, on the wall, anyway – take a good look around. If you find the corners of the room have assumed an unfamiliar rounded appearance you have not pressed the paper far enough into the corners. This is probably because you have tried to do too much at once. The paper should be cut so that it only goes about an inch past the corner. After all, you don't want to make the room any smaller than necessary.

That big bulge beside the door is the electric light switch. You should have cut a starred hole in the paper while it was still wet, to enable the paper to fit around the switch. It will be dry by this time and will not be easy. But you will still need to rescue it, or go over to gas.

If you have any large bubbles in the paper you can make an incision with a scalpel and pour in some paste, if you have any over. It may not be effective but it uses up the paste which is always a satisfaction to the parsimonious.

If there are any gaps between the lengths of paper it's a bit too late to do anything about it now. You should have eased them together while the paste was wet. Paper will always stretch a little. True, it makes matching the next piece a little more difficult, but time to worry about that when you come to it.

Well, there you are, the job is done. Apart from the little faults about which you may be over-critical, are you pleased with it? It is difficult enough to explain the sense of achievement which comes to a man when he looks around a room he has just finished papering. There is so much to show for it.

There's just one thing. You forgot to whiten the ceiling. And doesn't it show up! It will have to be done and isn't it going to make a mess of the new paper!

Nine

Making a Garden Swing

In case the title should inspire irrelevant thoughts or suggest a flippant comment or two, let it be known that this chapter has nothing to do with modernising the garden itself. It refers to that innocent source of pleasure which, once upon a time, no self-respecting garden dare be without, but which in recent years seems to have joined the procession of once familiar delights which have disappeared from the domestic scene, like rocking-horses, catapults, bees' wine and recitations.

But make no mistake about it, swings are as popular with children today as ever they were. If you don't believe it, and are not upset by the sight of blood, assemble four or five children around one swing and watch them decide who shall be first.

Undoubtedly, the simplest form of swing is one suspended from the convenient branch of a tree. All you need in that case is some rope and a wooden seat. The tree is unlikely to be uprooted by the most enthusiastic swinger and the only problem may arise from the chafing and consequent weakening of the rope.

Still, with a little forward planning you need not be present when the eventual calamity occurs and the tears will have dried and the wounds have been satisfactorily dressed by the time you appear. So this is a calculated risk you must be prepared to take.

'this solution **does** *require a tree'*

However, this solution *does* require a tree and they are not easily come by, and even when they are you cannot always be sure they will possess a convenient branch. If you are not in a hurry you can, of course, plant a suitable tree and wait for it to grow. But in this case you will either need to allow for a large seat since the child will have grown with the tree, or to persevere with your procreation so that there will always be a suitable child available at each stage of the tree's growth.

There is an alternative and it is with this alternative that we are about to concern ourselves – the erection of an orthodox swing.

This need not be an elaborate structure – two uprights,

a cross bar, two ropes and a seat are the component parts. But, all the same, some thought should be given to their assembly.

First of all consider well the siting of the swing. It should not be placed near a path in such a way that the user's feet or counterpart swing across it – unless the other members of the family are agile or don't mind being roughly prodded when they are not.

Nor should it be erected on the lawn, if the lawn is one in which you or your wife take a pride, since the area surrounding the swing soon gives up the unequal contest with scuffing feet, and leaves a large, bald, brown scar which never seems to heal even after the children grow up – and especially when they bring their own offspring to follow in their footsteps.

On the other hand, there are lawns which could only be improved by such cavalier treatment and if yours is one your troubles are over.

Again, if the lawn is the only convenient site, or if your objections are finally overruled, you could lay crazy paving around the swing area. But this does tend to lengthen the whole job, and if you haven't laid crazy paving before you have two problems instead of one and it might not be the paving that ends up crazy.

Having decided upon the site, your next job is a trip to your old friend in the do-it-yourself shop, if he sells the larger type of timber. If not, you visit the nearest timber yard.

For the posts you need something really stout, say 4″ x 3″, and since 'stout' also means 'heavy' arrange to have it delivered. You got into enough trouble with the hardboard and you might not get away with it so easily this time.

The length of these posts will, in the main, be decided by the length of rope you propose to use, but remember that a substantial portion of each post must be sunk into the ground. Within reason, the deeper the better, for unless your children are different from all others the posts will need all the support they can get. It is also advisable to bed the submerged part of the posts in concrete for much the same reason.

For the crossbar you don't need anything as bulky as the posts, just as long as it is strong enough to take the weight of at least two children in conflict. It must also be long enough to stretch from one post to the other, and if you think this is stating the obvious – just you wait and see.

The only other materials you require are a piece of board for the seat (the size dictated by the anatomical requirements only you will know), two lengths of rope or chain, and four large screw-eyes for connecting the rope to the seat and crossbar. In the event of chain being used, bolts may be better for this purpose.

Now that you have all the necessary equipment the toughest part of the job awaits you – digging the holes.

It doesn't matter how many times you drive an exploratory rod into the ground to find a suitable location, when you come to dig the actual hole you will almost immediately strike rock. Not immediately but *almost* immediately, so that you will already have gone too far to make a change of site feasible. The presence of rock usually means that its removal will result in a much larger hole than you either intended or required, not to mention your reduction to a trembling (and possibly blaspheming), physical wreck. And that's only the *first* hole.

By the time the second is dug half your lawn will have disappeared under excavated soil, rocks, builder's rubble and abandoned meat bones. The children will have carried a fair proportion of it through the lounge and upstairs, and your wife will be standing at the breakfast-room window with arms folded and wearing that overcast countenance you know so well.

Never mind, the holes are ready and the bottoms of the posts are well soaked in creosote – I hope. So you didn't think? So you'd better do it right away.

Now to mix the concrete to bed the posts in. You forgot to get any cement? Ah, well, he'll be glad to see you back at his shop again, but make sure you buy enough to complete the job, and don't forget the sand. Looking at the holes again you'll need about half a ton of concrete in each unless you board off part of the holes and replace some of the soil, which in the interests of everything and everybody, would be my advice.

By the time you return from the shop the shape and size of the holes will have changed a little as the children have been playing at trench warfare in your absence. So out comes the spade again.

I assume you know how to mix concrete, but in case the proportions have momentarily escaped you, a suitable mix would be 1 part cement, 2 parts sand, 4 parts gravel and 10 parts perspiration. Mix this to a fairly firm consistency and then bed it firmly around the base of the posts which should be held upright by the best method

'that overcast countenance you know so well'

available. Without knowing what equipment you have at hand it is difficult to make any suggestions, but the obvious one is most tiring, particularly with two posts at the same time.

There is no reason why the crossbar cannot be fixed to the posts now; in fact it will help to keep them upright. It can be nailed or screwed to them or, if you wish to show off your carpentry skill, you can make a halved joint with a strong bolt to secure both parts.

Now before bothering about the ropes and seat, and

especially before the concrete sets, step back and take a critical look at your handywork. You just didn't think, did you? I know I said 'the deeper the better' but I also said 'within reason'.

I agree that once the concrete sets, short of a bulldozer, nothing in the world will move those posts, not even the little roughneck next door. But then it shouldn't, should it, with six feet sunk into the ground? But who on earth can use a swing three feet high except, perhaps, the little garden gnome?

Better pull up those posts while the concrete is still soft, re-insert them with a maximum of three feet below the surface, and leave them until the concrete is quite hard, which process can be assisted by not testing it with a prodding stick every hour or so.

When the concrete has set firm you can proceed to hang the swing. The screw-eyes should be screwed one on either side of the crossbar, but not so near the edge that the knuckles of the hands holding the ropes are skinned on the posts.

Similarly, screw-eyes should be screwed into the seat, ensuring that each is in the precise centre of each side so that the seat does not tilt and eject the user immediately upon sitting.

Next, attach one end of each rope to the screw-eyes in the crossbar, securing as firmly as your affection for your children justifies. Then attach the opposite ends of the ropes to the screw-eyes in the seat, allowing sufficient length of rope to permit the swinger's legs to clear the ground, but not so much that you are called from the comfort of your chair every few minutes to lift the little

'tuck their feet up under the seat'

dear on and off. Tie off securely.

What a pity both pieces of rope are not the same length. Half an inch wouldn't have mattered much – but *four inches* is a bit steep, in more senses than one, and the movement along the seat may well induce splinters. So something must be done.

You can either build up the seat on one side or shorten the longer rope. Your decision will probably depend upon how securely you have fastened the rope.

Now that the swing is properly hung it shows up something else. The upright posts are not upright. They lean towards the hydrangeas – quite a bit. This means that if the swingers spread their legs their feet are likely to hit the left-hand post once every 'to' and once ever 'fro'. Ah, well, they'll just have to remember to tuck their feet up under the seat. It won't take long to form the habit. One thing is certain, now that the concrete is set nothing is going to induce it to part with the posts.

One final job remains, to 'make good' the area surrounding the swing. This means ramming as much of the removed soil as possible into the remains of the holes and hiding the surplus wherever your ingenuity and darkness suggest. If you remembered to retain the turf removed before digging the holes, this can now be fitted around the base of the swing and as much as possible of the remaining earth brushed off the grass.

This may sound a fairly simple task but it is possibly the most dangerous adventure you have ever embarked upon.

Don't forget the swing is now in full and violent use and never before have you been so prone to having a mischief done to you.

And don't expect any sympathy from your wife when you go in nursing your latest calamity. She has been hard at it for the last hour trying to get the mud off the carpets.

Still, the children are happy.

Ten

Repairing a Wooden Fence

One morning sooner or later, after a sleepless night spent listening to next door's garden gate crashing monotonously against the gate-post in the gale that threatened to rip away the roof over your head, you will draw the curtains to see your garden fence lying in a splintered wreck on top of your favourite rose bushes, or leaning at such an angle as to make no difference.

It is always *your* fence. It couldn't be the other one along the path, which is your neighbour's responsibility, it must be *yours*.

Now if the fence happened to divide your garden from that of an attractive blonde you might be tempted to postpone repairs indefinitely. But the decision isn't yours, is it? So there will be an insistent voice (not your conscience, either) urging immediate action.

But there rarely is a blonde. More likely a dyspeptic army-surplus who had occasion to complain the previous week about the smoke from your bonfire invading his garden, to which you replied . . . .

Yes, a bit impetuous, weren't you? You'd like to be able to repair the fence from his side, wouldn't you? But he's not going to be very accommodating, is he? So you've got to manage the best you can from your side.

Since there is no alternative to trampling on the rose bed it is going to get into a bit of a mess. Resign yourself

'the smoke from your bonfire'

to this from the outset and it will save you much heart-
ache.

Let us assume it is the arris rails which have parted
company with the posts. If they are rotten they will need
renewing; if they are sound everywhere except at the site
of the fracture it is possible to purchase special brackets to
secure them to the posts again, and this is a most

economical way out.

If the panel is not too big it may be possible to secure the palings to the arris rails and then fix the whole panel into position with the brackets. This is not easy if there is an unfriendly wind blowing or if no one is available to steady one end of the panel.

In the latter case the palings should be detached from the arris rails, if they have not already parted company, and the rails fixed to the posts with the brackets. The palings are then nailed to the rails in position. The problem is that they have to be nailed from old Grumpy's side which, in the prevailing circumstances, means hanging over the fence, with the blood flooding your brain, hammering at nails (including your own) with the hammer at full stretch. You will require four times the number of nails you would normally need as every nail dropped falls on enemy soil and is beyond reclamation.

This rather undignified exercise is made even more distasteful by the knowledge that your every movement is being carefully observed from behind the lace curtains of next door's kitchen window. Not to mention the fact that Grumpy's cocker spaniel is convinced you are invading his master's territory and does his best to discourage you by barking and growling, alternated with savage lunges at your extremely vulnerable head.

You enjoy a short respite when his slavering jaws eventually close on the brim of your favourite gardening hat. Perhaps 'enjoy' is not the right word since that hat really was your favourite and you know that if ever it is rescued it will never be the same again – not after he has finished with it. Still it does enable you to drive home the

'Pity you had to lose your balance'

last few nails without that prickly feeling at the back of your neck.

It's good to straighten up at last and step away from your cramped position at the fence where you have been concentrating on avoiding damage to your border.

Careful now! Too late! You just had to step back into the middle of that rose bush. Pity you had to lose your balance as well, though, and most unfortunate that the rose happened to be 'Peace' with its inch-thick shoots and thorns like harpoon barbs.

Your cries bring all your neighbours to their windows

and a flush of pleasure to the face of old Grumpy. And it's even more painful getting off the rose bush than it was getting on – more prolonged, too. You'd have thought your wife would have come to your assistance, though. Still, she's got the wireless on a bit loud – or is she still feeling sore with you? Anyway, the children arrive hotfoot. They wouldn't miss it for anything.

When you've recovered – no hurry, a couple of days' time will do – take another look at the fence. See where you've gone wrong? Yes, the nails you used were too long. They are sticking through more than an inch.

It wouldn't have mattered so much the other way, but they are sticking out *your* side of the fence. They won't be very funny when you start pruning or weeding. So now you will either have to bend them over with a hammer or nip off the ends with a pair of pincers.

So much for the broken arris rail, but supposing a post had snapped off. Well, then you'd have all the foregoing as well as digging out the root of the old post and digging in a new one. It will also probably mean that you will have to replace two panels of fencing instead of one.

Don't be surprised, either to find that old Grumpy has nailed his favourite rambler to your post and despite the fact that it is *your* fence, he's going to be pretty annoyed if any harm comes to his roses during repairs.

It would be grand if it were possible to pull the stump of the old post straight out of the ground leaving a nice, snug hole to receive the new one. But life is not like that. When anything has been in the earth as long as your post has, the earth assumes all proprietary rights and refuses to surrender ownership without a life-and-death struggle.

119

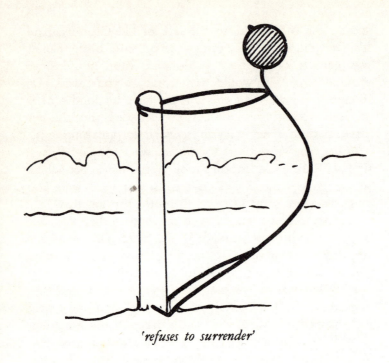

'refuses to surrender'

This you will discover for yourself when you try to release the earth's grip on the post. The surrounding area will resemble a battlefield long before you are justified in claiming a victory, and the neat little hole you had hoped to leave will be more like a bomb crater. But try to prevent that crater from encroaching on the next garden or hostilities may well be extended.

The replacement post can either be of wood or concrete. If you prefer to stick to timber then it should be of hard wood, such as oak, which is extremely heavy

120

to handle and next to impossible to drive nails or screws into.

The post should be well soaked in creosote and allowed to dry before being planted. When brushing on the creosote it is advisable to cover yourself up as though about to tackle a swarm of bees, for creosote is the most perverse liquid ever concocted and delights in splashing at you from the most unexpected angles and with untiring persistence.

When dry, the post should be positioned in the hole, as near as possible in line with the remaining posts. This is not as easy as it might be since the hole is now considerably larger than the one the old post occupied. A variety of different positions are available – all wrong except one.

When the final position is selected, surround the base with freshly mixed concrete as you did when erecting the swing, and allow it to set hard before fixing the arris rails. This will also allow time to try to remove the corrugations from your back.

From here on the procedure is as for the broken arris rail, except that you are not feeling nearly as fresh and you've already lost your favourite garden hat.

If you decide upon a concrete post you don't have to bother about creosoting which, be assured, is a consideration. Also, of course, you will be spiking the guns of old Grumpy who will no longer be able to nail his rambler to your post.

Eleven

In Conclusion

This is the point at which I begin to have doubts. For it is here that I abandon you to your own devices and I wonder whether it might not have been kinder, or perhaps wiser, to have left you in ignorance, to discover for yourself the problems and pitfalls that beset the path which now lies ahead.

For in the previous pages I have only fingered the fringes of the subject which, like the iceberg, conceals in menacing silence its greater and more dangerous bulk.

I try to find some consolation in the thought that I have protected you from at least the more obvious blunders, and robbed the unpleasanter experiences of their element of surprise. But have I, by omission, led you into a sense of false security, thinking that you now know it all and are fully equipped to tackle any challenge with which your wife may confront you?

I do hope not, for there is always the possibility that one day our paths may cross and I don't like unpleasant surprises, either.

So let me plead with you to treat this book as a *primer* only. You have much still to learn and, in the main, it will be the direct result of experience – mostly painful. And as at the end of each job you count your fingers again and sigh with relief (or resignation) at the tally – don't forget there will be another job tomorrow.

If, however, you have managed to read this book without anyone finding out, now is the time to be brave and resolute, if you've got what it takes. Sooner or later you will learn for yourself that the happiest man on earth is the one of whom his wife never tires of saying: 'He's hopeless about the house. Doesn't know one end of a hammer from the other!'